GUITAR FOR GIRLS

A Beginner's Guide to Playing Acoustic & Electric Guitar

BY ALI HANDAL

ISBN 978-1-4584-0845-7

PLAYBACK+
Speed • Pitch • Balance • Loop

The price of this book includes access to audio tracks online, for download or streaming, using the unique code below. The tracks provide an audio demonstration of each example in the book performed by the author.

Now including *PLAYBACK+*, a multi-functional audio player that allows you to slow down audio without changing pitch, set loop points, change keys, pan left or right — available exclusively from Hal Leonard.

To access audio visit:
www.halleonard.com/mylibrary

Enter Code
3878-8148-9543-8079

HAL•LEONARD® CORPORATION

7777 W. BLUEMOUND RD. P.O. BOX 13819 MILWAUKEE, WI 53213

Visit Hal Leonard Online at
www.halleonard.com

INTRODUCTION

Guitar for Girls is designed for girls (and girls at heart!) who are learning to play guitar. I hope you find this guide really fun and easy to use. You'll be learning lots of fantastic songs that have been sung, and primarily written, by female artists in many different styles of music. It's my hope that you'll find some new favorite artists to dive into, and that you'll enjoy exploring your own creativity using the tools in this book.

If you're a budding singer/songwriter yourself, there are *lots* of tools in this book to help you stand out from the crowd, including many unique chord alternatives and techniques to keep your guitar playing (and your songwriting) fresh.

You may be relieved to know that you don't need to know *any* music theory in order to learn guitar, or to use this book. However, it's my hope that you'll develop such a love for music that your natural curiosity will spur you on to learn *everything* you can about it, including the finer points of music theory. The more you know about how music works, the more tools you have in your arsenal, and the easier it is to communicate and command respect from your fellow musicians.

A few tips on how to approach learning the songs in this book:

- Listen to the example recording before you try to play each example yourself.
- Listen to the original artist's rendition of the song you're learning, as well as other artists' versions (you can find these by searching for the songs on iTunes or other music sites).
- Visit www.AliHandal.com/Lessons for extra content and video lessons.
- And most importantly,

TURN IT UP AND HAVE FUN!

~Ali

CHAPTER ONE:

LET'S GET STARTED!

"I want every girl in the world to pick up a guitar and start screaming." ~Courtney Love

PARTS OF THE GUITAR

CONGRATULATIONS on your decision to learn to play guitar! The guitar is an incredibly versatile instrument, and, if you've ever been to a music store, you know that there are many types of guitars to choose from. You can start learning on either an acoustic or an electric guitar—they're both tuned the same way and contain the same notes. An acoustic guitar, though a bit rougher on the fingers at first, is a great place to start (and when you do pick up an electric guitar, it'll feel so easy to play in comparison!). If you want to start on electric, that's cool too; just know that you'll also need to invest in an amplifier so you can hear yourself rock out.

Before you begin playing, make sure to check out the diagrams and familiarize yourself with the different parts of the acoustic and electric guitar. Feel free to flip back to this page as you read, since we'll be referencing these parts of your guitar throughout the book.

ELECTRIC GUITAR

» TUNING KEYS

» NUT

» HEADSTOCK

» FRETS

» PICKUPS

» VOLUME CONTROL

» TREMOLO BAR

» PICKUP SELECTOR SWITCH

» TONE CONTROLS

» OUTPUT JACK

» STRAP BUTTON

BRIDGE

PICK GUARD

SOUND HOLE

NECK & FINGERBOARD

BODY

"My various guitars have different voices and they function as my singing and writing partners. The unique qualities of a guitar's voice have a real effect on what comes out."

~Ani DiFranco

POSTURE

While you're first learning to play, you'll probably be seated most of the time you practice. Whether you sit or stand, here are some basic guidelines:

- Choose a comfortable chair with no armrests. Make sure your feet easily reach the ground (or a footstool) so you can rest the guitar securely on your lap.

- Balance your weight evenly from left to right, sit up straight, and keep as much tension out of your entire body as possible.

- If you start to feel tension (which often happens when you're concentrating on learning new skills and songs), take a few moments to relax and then adjust your position.

- Tilt the guitar's neck upward (not downward).

- Avoid the temptation to angle the topside of the guitar up and toward you to see the fretboard better. Ultimately, it's best to be able to play the guitar without having to look at the fretboard too often. With consistent practice, you'll be able to do it. In the meantime, keep your guitar as vertical as possible.

PITCH

The six strings of the guitar are ordered from the highest-sounding string to the lowest (closest to your head). These differences in the lowness and highness of a sound are called *pitch*. Each string is tuned to a particular sound, or pitch, when *open* (not *fretted*, or pressed down). In order from highest (string 1) to lowest (string 6), these pitches are E-B-G-D-A-E. Strike each string in turn and notice the different sound each one makes.

THE FRETBOARD

Each guitar string is named after the pitch it sounds when you play it open (without fretting it). The highest-pitched string (the thinnest one) is tuned to E and is often called the *high E* string, or the first string. The next string is tuned to B and called the B string, or the second string. Next is the G, or third string; then the D, or fourth string; then the A, or fifth string. Lastly is the sixth string (the thickest), commonly called the *low E* string.

Notice that different pitches are produced when you press on each string at different frets. When a string is pressed at the frets located "lower" on the neck (toward the nut), the sound is lower; when the same string is pressed at the frets located "higher" on the neck (toward the bridge), the sound is higher.

▶▶ Standing Up

When you play guitar standing up, you'll need to use a shoulder strap. While some of the coolest rock stars out there play with their guitars slung super-low, when you adjust the length of *your* guitar strap, please make sure that the guitar is set at a level that's comfortable for *you* to play. Remember that everyone is built differently— your arms may not be as long as a 30-year-old male rock star's, and trying to play your guitar while it's slung around your knees can be dangerous for your wrist health (not to mention very hard to do!). As a general rule, always make sure that every part of your body feels comfortable while playing so as to minimize any chance of injury.

"All I've done is point out that you need to be yourself and that's rock and roll."
~Chrissie Hynde

▶▶ Easy Way To Memorize Your String Names!

String 1: **E**very

String 2: **B**old

String 3: **G**irl

String 4: **D**eserves

String 5: **A**n

String 6: **E**ncore

TUNING

Each time before you play, it's important to make sure that your guitar is *in tune*—that is, that all of your strings are set to the proper pitch. In order to adjust the pitch of your strings, you may need to loosen or tighten them with the tuning pegs, or *tune* them. You have several options for tuning your guitar…

Electronic Tuner

Until you're more familiar with correct pitch, using an electronic tuner is a great, reliable option. These tuners sense the pitch produced from a plucked open string and indicate whether the pitch is correct, *flat* (too low), or *sharp* (too high). Using the tuning pegs, you then either tighten or loosen the string until the meter on the electronic tuner indicates that the pitch is correct.

Piano/Keyboard

If you have a (tuned!) piano or keyboard available, and you know where "middle C" is located, you can tune your guitar strings by ear according to the sound of the corresponding note on the keyboard. This can be a challenging way to tune at first, but it can also be a good way to practice hearing differences in pitch. Similarly, you can also use the tuning notes on Track 1 as reference pitches.

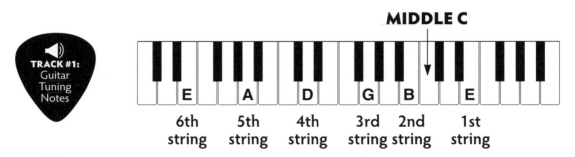

Relative Tuning

Another way to tune your guitar by ear is to do so in relation to your guitar's other strings.

 Tune the sixth string E to a piano, a pitch pipe, or an electronic tuner. If none of the above is available, approximate E the best you can.

 Press the sixth string at the 5th fret, which is the note A. Tune the open fifth string to this pitch.

Press the fifth string at the 5th fret, which is the note D. Tune the open fourth string to this pitch.

Press the fourth string at the 5th fret, which is the note G. Tune the open third string to this pitch.

Press the third string at the 4th fret, which is the note B. Tune the open second string to this pitch.

Press the second string at the 5th fret, which is the note E. Tune the open first string to this pitch.

Take Your Time Tuning!

There are few things more unpleasant than hearing an out-of-tune guitar, so make sure you take time to tune your guitar before you start playing. You'll be doing your audience's ears (and your own) a favor, and you'll be training your ears to hear what chords sound like when they're played precisely in tune. This is great for developing your overall musicality.

Remember, when using the relative tuning or keyboard/piano methods:

⦿ Always turn the tuning peg slowly so that you can clearly discern the change in pitch that results from this adjustment. You may also need to pluck and adjust the string a few times before getting to the correct pitch.

⦿ Listen for a series of pulsating *beat waves*. These indicate how far or close you are to the correct pitch. The farther you are from the exact pitch, the faster the beat waves; the closer you are, the slower the beat waves. When the beat waves stop completely, you've arrived at the correct pitch.

⦿ Always tune a string up towards the correct pitch, rather than down. Start by tuning your string below the desired pitch, and then gradually tune up until you reach the correct pitch. Doing this will stretch the string into place and help it stay in tune longer.

HANDS

Left-Hand (or Fretting Hand) Position

Throughout this book, you'll see directions as to which fingers should be placed at which points on the fretboard. Nearly all guitar instructional books use the same method for naming your fingers, as shown in the photo below.

Learning correct left-hand placement is important to your overall hand health and playing skill. Check out the photos below for examples of healthy left-hand placement.

Right-Hand (or Picking Hand) Position

How you position your right hand varies, depending on whether you're using a pick or playing with your fingers. This book focuses primarily on using a pick.

Playing with a Pick

You'll usually use a pick (or a *plectrum*, if you want to get fancy about it) to strike the strings. The best way to hold a pick is to grip it between your thumb and index finger while keeping the rest of your hand relaxed and your fingers curved (including your index finger). To accomplish this, try bending

your index finger and placing your thumb on the side of the first knuckle (kind of like when you hold a key to open your front door). Next, grab the pointy end of the pick with your left hand and slide the opposite end of the pick between your thumb and index finger, while keeping them in position. Push the pick in far enough so that only the tip of the pick is showing. Don't squeeze too hard, but do keep your hold on the pick just firm enough so you don't drop the pick when you hit the strings. You can keep your other three fingers tucked into the palm of your hand, fanned out, or resting on the body of the guitar.

You can pick each string one at a time, or *strum* several of them together. To start, try strumming several strings at once in a downward motion (a *downstroke*). Practice your downstroke to get the feel of the pick against the strings. Strum with enough force to create a solid and steady sound, but not so hard that your pick bends or gets caught between strings. Next, try picking each string, one by one, from bottom to top. Practice this until it feels comfortable. Finally, try reversing your direction to produce an *upstroke*, or upward strum of all the strings.

As you learn to play the chords and songs in the book, you'll be strumming the strings with downstrokes and upstrokes in different rhythmic patterns. Listening to the accompanying audio will help you get these strum patterns in your hands and ears.

Place your thumb on the underside of the guitar neck.

Arch your fingers so you'll be able to reach all the strings more easily.

2ND

3RD

1ST

4TH

T

PRACTICE HABITS

"I think I've become a much better singer and a much better player. Years and years of playing a couple of hours every day will do that."

~Sarah McLachlan

How Much Should I Practice?

The amount of time you practice is less important than the consistency with which you practice. Meaning, you'll see more progress if you practice 30 minutes a day for six days a week than if you practice one day a week for four hours

at a time. When you're first starting out, you may want to break up your practice sessions into smaller chunks (e.g., 10 or 15 minutes at a time). If your initial goal is to practice for 30 minutes a day, you could play for ten minutes in the morning, ten minutes in the afternoon, and ten minutes in the evening. This is an especially good strategy in the beginning, when your fingers get sore quickly (and when you may get frustrated easily). With consistent practicing, you'll build up your hand strength so that you can play for longer periods of time without needing a break.

No matter if you're a beginner or an advanced performer, though, *always* listen to your body and take breaks when you need to! If you practice through wrist or hand pain without resting your muscles, you put yourself at risk for injury, which can prevent you from playing. In the long run, it's much better to take as many breaks as you need to in order to stay healthy. That way, you'll have many, many years of playing ahead of you!

Warming Up

Warming up for a practice session or performance will help you play better and help guard against injuries such as muscle strain, or more serious problems such as *tendonitis* (inflammation of a tendon caused by repetitive motion and overexertion).

First, you'll want to get the blood flowing to your hands. You can do this by repeatedly making a fist and then relaxing your hands, or by waving your arms in the air. Try any gentle movements you can think of to get the blood pumping to your fingers.

A warm-up routine on guitar can be as simple as slowly playing random notes all around the fretboard. After that you can play a few chords and rhythms. The main thing to remember is to start playing gently, slowly, and precisely. This helps get your hands "in sync," and establishes a precedent of precision that you can carry through your entire practice session.

 Beware of Practice Exaggerators

Lots of folks go on and on about the hundreds of hours they're practicing each week. While it *may* be true that they're playing for 10+ hours a day and sleeping with their guitars in their arms, it *also* may be true that they're spending at least a few of those hours playing video games with their guitars sitting next to them, getting distracted by the phone, or... you get the picture. Just because they say it, doesn't mean it's true. So before you risk injury from over-practicing just to keep up with your friends or with what you've heard about your favorite guitar players, just know that it's possible to become a great player and also have a life.

CHAPTER TWO:
INTRODUCING CHORDS

"I think there's nothing better than seeing a three-chord, straight-up rock 'n' roll band in your face with sweaty music and three-minute, good songs" ~Joan Jett

WHAT'S A CHORD?

CHORDS are the very heart and soul of guitar playing. With just a few chords under your belt, you can accompany yourself while you sing your favorite songs, and you can write your own songs too!

A *chord* can be defined as playing a group of three or more notes at the same time. Most guitar chords use four, five, or all six strings, and you'll place several fingers on different frets at the same time. At first, this can be challenging, but with practice and patience, you'll be playing plenty of chords and full songs in no time.

What's an Open Chord?

The fastest way to start playing songs on your guitar is to learn some *open chords*. Open chords, also known as open-position chords, are played on the first few frets of the guitar. They're called "open" because they use at least one open (non-fretted) string, and the other strings are fretted on either the first, second, third, or fourth fret.

What's a Chord Diagram?

Take a close look at your guitar's fingerboard. Note the horizontal divisions that run its entire length. These divisions are the guitar's *frets*. Frets are numbered from 1–22 and run from "low" on the neck (just below the nut), to "high" (where the neck and body are joined). We'll show sections of frets throughout this book via *chord diagrams*, which are vertical representations of the guitar's fingerboard.

The six vertical lines of the chord diagram represent your guitar's strings: low E, A, D, G, B, and high E, from left to right. The thick horizontal line at the top represents your guitar's nut, and the thin horizontal lines are your guitar's frets.

In the chord diagram, you'll see dots on the fretboard to show where your fingers go, as well as numbers (from 1 to 4, and sometimes "T" for thumb) at the bottom to show which fingers to use. If the chord uses open strings, you'll see an open circle, "O," just above the string that should be played open. And if any strings should not be played in the chord, an "X" appears above that string.

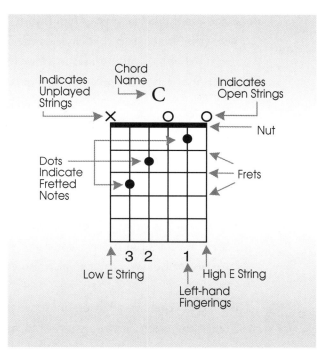

The *chord symbol*, which tells you the name of the chord, is written above the chord diagram. If the chord symbol is a single, capital letter (e.g., "C"), then the chord is major. A good description for the sound of a major chord is "happy," "positive," or "bright."

If a lower-case "m" appears in the chord symbol (e.g., "Am"), the chord is minor. A good description for the tonal quality of a minor chord is "sad," "dark," or "melancholy." There are lots of other chord types besides major and minor, but because these two are the most common, we'll start with them for now.

YOUR FIRST CHORD: Am

It's time to learn your first chord! Here's the chord diagram for an A minor chord:

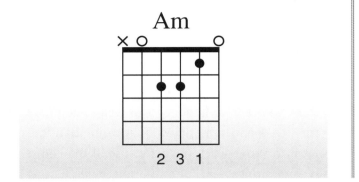

Notice on the chord diagram that the A and high E strings are open, the low E string is not played, and the D, G, and B strings are fretted at the 1st and 2nd frets. At first, start slowly and fret each string one at a time. With practice, you'll be able to place all of your left-hand fingers on the correct frets in one fell swoop, but it'll take some time, so have patience with yourself!

Let's walk through playing your first A minor chord:

 Place the fingertip of your first (index) finger on the 1st fret of the B string—not on the actual *fret wire* (the metal strip that divides the frets), but just behind it, toward the nut. Don't press down too hard yet—wait until your other fingers are in position. Apply just enough pressure to keep your finger in position while you move to the next finger in step 2.

 Moving to the D string, place your second (middle) finger on the 2nd fret of the D string.

③ On the G string, place your third (ring) finger on the 2nd fret. You might notice that you need to move your second finger toward the nut so you can squeeze your third finger into place.

④ Now, press down *firmly* on the three fretted strings with the top parts of your fingertips. Make sure that your fingers are arched and your fingertips are coming straight down onto the fretboard (see photo below). You can also use your thumb for leverage by squeezing the back of the neck.

⑤ Now that you have all three fingers in place, make sure that your fingers aren't touching any strings except the ones they're assigned to, and strum downward across strings 5 through 1 using either a pick or your picking hand's thumb. Congratulations! You've just played your first chord!

 Finger Placement

Though it's usually best to place your fingers just behind the fret wire, with some chords, you'll have to move a finger or two to the middle of the fret area. A good example is the A minor chord, which requires the second finger to fret the D string in the middle of the 2nd-fret area.

"I think I'm constantly in a state of adjustment."
~Patti Smith

Hmmm… That Didn't Sound Right!

"The failures and successes are necessary for learning."
~Wynonna Judd

If your chord sounds a bit "out" (or just plain crummy!), don't worry—that's perfectly normal when you're just starting! Here are a few things to check that will help you get your chords sounding gorgeous:

- **Is your guitar in tune?** This is the number one reason why chords sound unpleasant. Re-check your tuning. If even one string is slightly out of tune, your whole chord will sound bad.

- **Are your fingers pushing down hard enough on the strings?** If you don't press down hard enough, your fretted notes will either buzz or make no sound at all. Lift your fingers off the fretboard and check out your fingertips. If you don't see a little groove in your fingertip, you aren't pressing hard enough!

- **Are you bending the strings out of tune?** A common problem that can be tricky to see but easy to hear, is pushing the strings out of place (either toward the ceiling or floor) when you fret them. When you push a string out of place (which often happens when you push a little *too* hard), the string goes out of tune, making the whole chord sound out of tune. To avoid this, make sure you press each string straight down against the fretboard.

- **Are you accidentally muting the strings?** Make sure none of your fretting fingers are touching any surrounding strings. Touching surrounding strings with your fingers will keep them from ringing out, causing a muted tone, or sometimes no tone at all.

New Chord Practice Tip

"Put time into learning your craft. It seems like people want success so quickly, way before they're ready."
~Lucinda Williams

In the beginning, and anytime you're learning to play a difficult chord, it can be very helpful to play the chord as an *arpeggio* (playing the notes of the chord one at a time and in sequence). Slowly pluck (or pick) each string individually, and listen carefully. Can you hear the string ring out absolutely clear, or do you hear some dullness or a buzzing sound? If a note doesn't sound clear, one of several things may be happening. You may not be pressing down hard enough on the fretboard, you may be using too much of your fingertip to press down on the string, or your hand may be inadvertently touching the strings. Reposition your fingers and press the strings firmly until you can pluck the string and hear the note 100% clearly. Continue to pluck each string of the chord in this way, correcting any "fuzzy" notes as you go, until you have your fretting hand positioned in such a way that every note of the chord rings out 100% clearly. Yes, it's tedious, but this attention to detail is what will make your guitar playing great. Plus, it's *way* more fun to play when you can hear all the notes!

Building Calluses

"Work through your calluses... practice to your favorite records. Find some friends to play with, just for fun. Practice, practice, practice!" ~Joan Jett

You may be finding out firsthand that learning to play the guitar can be a bit painful! In the beginning, your fingertips might hurt as you learn how hard you need to press down on the strings with your fretting fingers. In order to play without pain, you'll need to build up *calluses* (layers of dead skin) on your fingertips.

By practicing regularly, you'll build up calluses quickly, and the pain in your fingertips will start going away. How quickly you build up your calluses depends on how much and how often you practice. While it's great to practice a lot, you should *always* take a break when your fingers, wrist, or any other part of your body feels sore. It's a lot easier to avoid an overuse injury (e.g., muscle strain or tendonitis) than it is to get rid of one. You'll get to practice a lot more over time if you remain healthy and uninjured!

YOUR SECOND CHORD: E

One of the most frequently played and beloved chords on the guitar is E major. A very cool thing about this chord is that it's *exactly* the same shape as the A minor chord you just learned, only the whole shape is moved over one string (so instead of your first finger being on the B string, it's on the G string). Notice on the chord diagram that the low E, B, and high E strings are open in this chord, while the A, D, and G strings are fretted at the 2nd and 1st frets. Keeping this in mind, try playing an E major chord. If you have any trouble, just refer back to the troubleshooting tips for the A minor chord and apply them to the E major chord.

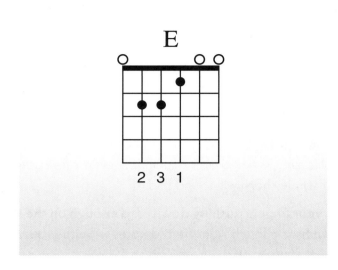

YOUR FIRST SONG: FEVER

"Fever" is a classic American standard that's been recorded by hundreds of artists over the years, including Peggy Lee, Bette Midler, Christina Aguilera, and Madonna (check out their recordings to hear how a great song can be interpreted differently by various artists).

This song uses both chords we just learned—the A minor for most of the verse, and the E at the end. Listen to the recording to hear how to time your strumming.

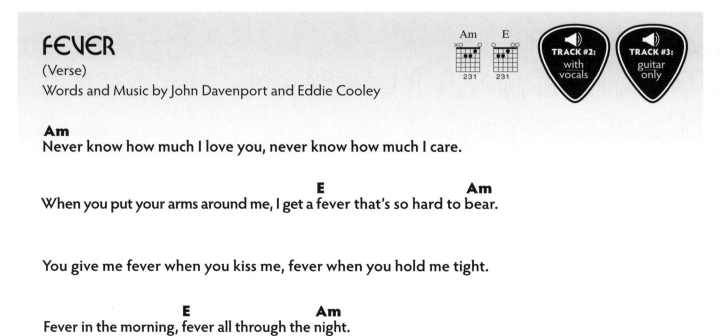

FEVER

(Verse)

Words and Music by John Davenport and Eddie Cooley

Am
Never know how much I love you, never know how much I care.

          E   **Am**
When you put your arms around me, I get a fever that's so hard to bear.

You give me fever when you kiss me, fever when you hold me tight.

  E   **Am**
Fever in the morning, fever all through the night.

≫ Standards

One of the marks of a classic song (often referred to as a "standard") is that it's been interpreted and recorded by many different musical artists—often in vastly different styles. For inspiration, check out some of the different versions of "Fever" that artists have recorded over the last 50+ years (there are literally hundreds of different versions and remixes on iTunes that you can sample).

Keep on Keeping on!

"Be true to yourself and believe in what you do and stick to it."

~Shawn Colvin

At first, your version of "Fever" won't sound anything like the famous professional recordings, but don't get intimidated or discouraged! Behind every hit recording are many musicians with *years* of experience behind them. Don't expect yourself to sound just like the recording when you're first starting out. Enjoy playing (and singing, if you like) as much as you can right now, and with practice you'll get better and better, eventually developing your own unique playing style.

Em CHORD

You'll like this chord—it's easier than the first two you learned! Put your middle finger on the A string at the 2nd fret, then put your ring finger on the D string at the 2nd fret. Now strum all six strings and you're playing an E minor chord!

A CHORD

The A major chord is played on the top five strings, and can feel a bit cramped until you get used to it. You have several choices of which finger to use on each string. Try all three listed under the chord diagram and use the one that's most comfortable for you.

D CHORD

This chord is played on the top four strings only, with an open D string. Place your first finger on the 2nd fret of the G string, your second finger on the 2nd fret of the high E string, and your third finger on the 3rd fret of the B string. Play the open D string, but do your best not to strike the low E and A strings (this will take some practice).

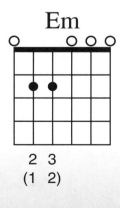

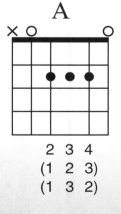

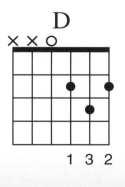

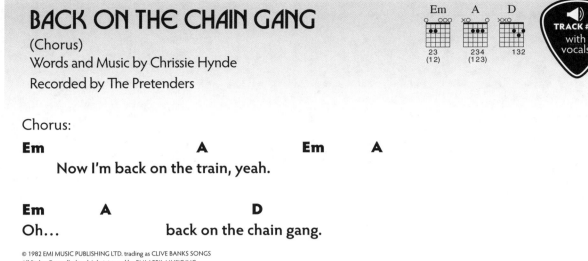

BACK ON THE CHAIN GANG

(Chorus)

Words and Music by Chrissie Hynde

Recorded by The Pretenders

Chorus:

Em   **A**   **Em**   **A**
    Now I'm back on the train, yeah.

Em   **A**   **D**
Oh…   back on the chain gang.

 Practice Tip: Leave Early, Arrive on Time

My very first guitar teacher taught me an important lesson when I was learning to play. He said that moving from chord to chord within a song is just like moving from place to place in real life. Sometimes, especially when you're not sure where you're going or how long it'll take you to get there, you need to leave early in order to arrive on time.

Musically, when the song you're playing involves a chord change (as most songs do), it's important to get to your next chord on time—that is, on the first beat the chord is supposed to be played. If you're late to play that chord, the song just won't sound right. So when you start learning to play a song, if you think it might take you a little while of fumbling around on the guitar neck in order to get your fingers into position for your next chord, that's okay. Just stop playing the chord you're on a little early, so you can make sure you play the next chord right on time. As you get more familiar with the chords and the songs you're playing, you can leave less and less early, and you'll still arrive at that next chord on time.

G CHORD

Good news, you have your choice in fingering for the open G chord. The first fingering will probably be easier because it doesn't utilize the typically weak pinky finger, but don't completely neglect learning the second fingering. Depending on which chord you're transitioning from or going to in the song you're playing, you may want to choose that second one.

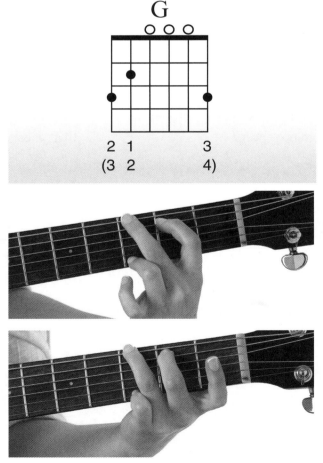

BACK ON THE CHAIN GANG

(Verse & Chorus)

Words and Music by Chrissie Hynde

Recorded by The Pretenders

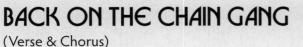

Verse:

D   **A**   **Em**   **G**
I found a picture of you…   oh…

D   **A**   **Em**   **G**
What hijacked my world that night,

D   **A**   **Em**   **G**
To a place in the past we've been cast out of… oh…

D   **A**   **Em**   **G**
Now we're back in the fight.

Chorus:

Em   **A**   **Em**   **A**
Now I'm back on the train, yeah.

Em   **A**   **D**
Oh…   back on the chain gang.

C CHORD

This chord can be a bit tricky. As you work on your finger placement, make sure they are arched enough so that each finger is *only* touching its assigned string. The G and high E strings must ring out freely (this will take a bit of practice). Let's start by placing your third finger on the A string at the 3rd fret, toward the front of the fret. Next, place your second finger on the D string at the 2nd fret. Lastly, place your first finger on the B string at the 1st fret.

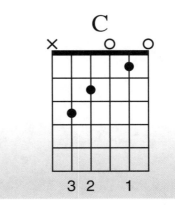

"My goal as an artist is to always be true to who I am and give my fans music they will enjoy for a lifetime." ~Faith Hill

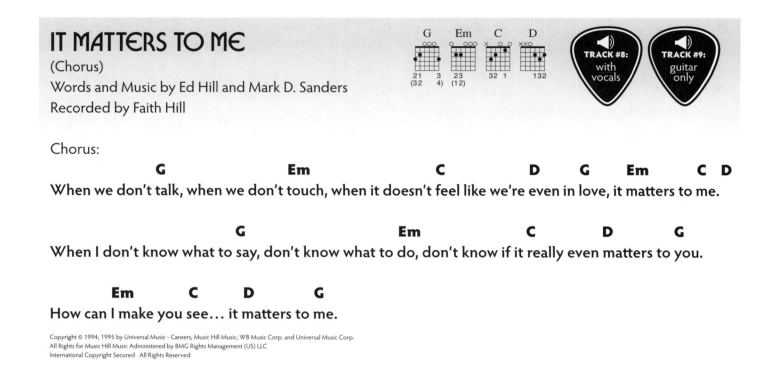

IT MATTERS TO ME

(Chorus)

Words and Music by Ed Hill and Mark D. Sanders

Recorded by Faith Hill

Chorus:

              G   **Em**   **C**   **D** **G**   **Em**   **C** **D**

When we don't talk, when we don't touch, when it doesn't feel like we're even in love, it matters to me.

            G   **Em**   **C**   **D**   **G**

When I don't know what to say, don't know what to do, don't know if it really even matters to you.

  Em   **C**   **D**   **G**

How can I make you see… it matters to me.

Alternate Version of the G Chord

Sometimes it sounds nice to play the open G major chord with all four fingers of the left hand, as shown here. Try it on "It Matters to Me" and notice that when you switch from the D major to the G major chord, you can keep your third finger where it is (the 3rd fret of the B string) for both chords. When moving to the G major chord, simply place your pinky on the 3rd fret of the high E string, move your first and second fingers into their proper places, and voila, you're playing G major! ■

CHAPTER THREE:
ADVANCED CHORDS

SUSPENDED CHORDS: Dsus4

A GOOD description for the tonal quality of a *suspended* chord (or "sus" chord) is "active," or "wanting to resolve" to a more stable chord (like a related major or minor chord). Let's look at one of the most commonly used suspended chords in popular guitar music: Dsus4.

When playing Dsus4 in a song, you'll often be playing the regular D major chord either right before it or right after it (or both). The easiest way to play this chord is to simply add your fourth finger to the D chord you already know (on the 3rd fret of the high E string), without even moving your second finger.

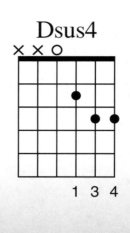

Dsus4

"Don't let anyone tell you that you have to be a certain way. Be unique. Be what you feel." ~Melissa Etheridge

COME TO MY WINDOW
(Verse & Chorus)
Words and Music by Melissa Etheridge
Recorded by Melissa Etheridge

| C | G | D | Dsus4 | Em | Am |

TRACK #10: with vocals
TRACK #11: guitar only

Verse:

C   **G**   **D**   **Dsus4**
I would dial the numbers just to listen to your breath,

   C   **G**   **D**   **Dsus4**
And I would stand inside my hell and hold the hand of death.

C   **G** **D**   **Dsus4**
You don't know how far I'd go to ease this precious ache,

   C   **G** **D**
And you don't know how much I'd give or how much I can take.

  Em   **C**   **D**   **Dsus4**   **Em**   **C**   **D**
Just to reach you,   just to reach you,   oh, to reach you.

Chorus:

G   **C** **Am** **D** **G**   **C** **Am**   **D**
  Come to my window.   Crawl inside, wait by the light of the moon.

G   **C** **Am** **D**   **G** **C** **Am**   **D** **G**
  Come to my window, I'll be home soon.

Asus4 CHORD

Another popular suspended chord is the Asus4 chord. Moving from the A major chord, you simply slide your fourth finger up one fret to the 3rd fret of the B string (when you're using the 2, 3, 4 fingering of your A major chord). In many songs, like the next one, you'll quickly alternate between A major and Asus4—listen to that effect and notice its particular sonic texture. Before you play the next tune, listen to the recorded example to hear the correct timing of the chord changes.

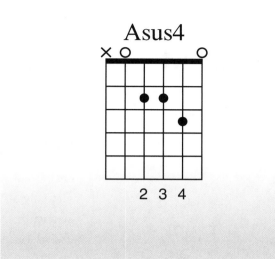

Asus4

"Where other people would rather go out and party, I would rather stay at home with my grand piano and candles and incense and a glass of wine and an idea." ~Stevie Nicks

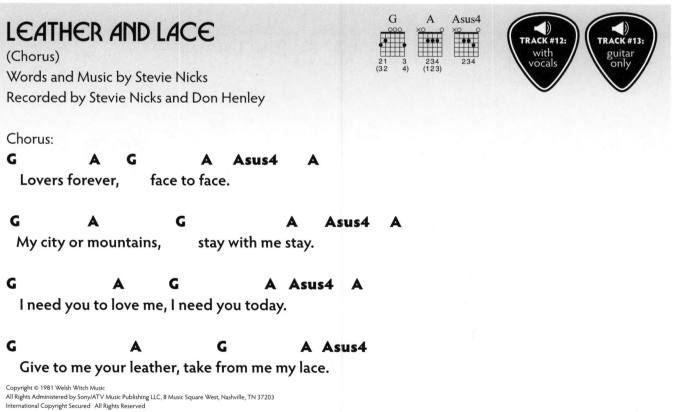

LEATHER AND LACE

(Chorus)

Words and Music by Stevie Nicks
Recorded by Stevie Nicks and Don Henley

Chorus:

G   A   G   A Asus4   A
  Lovers forever,   face to face.

G   A   G   A Asus4   A
  My city or mountains,   stay with me stay.

G   A   G   A Asus4   A
  I need you to love me, I need you today.

G   A   G   A Asus4
  Give to me your leather, take from me my lace.

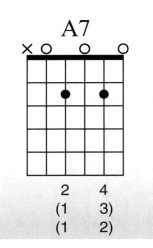

A7

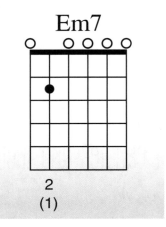

Em7

SEVENTH CHORDS

Seventh chords are colorful alternatives to basic major and minor chords and—bonus!—the ones you're learning here are easier to play than the basic chords they're related to! There are three types of seventh chords: *dominant seventh*, *minor seventh*, and *major seventh*.

DOMINANT SEVENTH CHORDS: A7

Dominant seventh chords have a funky, bluesy sound and are used in virtually all styles of music. Once you learn the A7 chord, compare its sound to the A major chord—there's only one note added to the A7 chord, but it makes a big difference in how the chord feels.

MINOR SEVENTH CHORDS: Em7

Minor seventh chords have a certain mystique to them. Sometimes they sound bittersweet, sometimes funky, and at times they're very pretty. A lot depends on the context of the song they're in, as well as the chords coming before and after. Here's an Em7 chord—the easiest chord in the book to play!

"It's important to give it all you have while you have the chance." ~Shania Twain

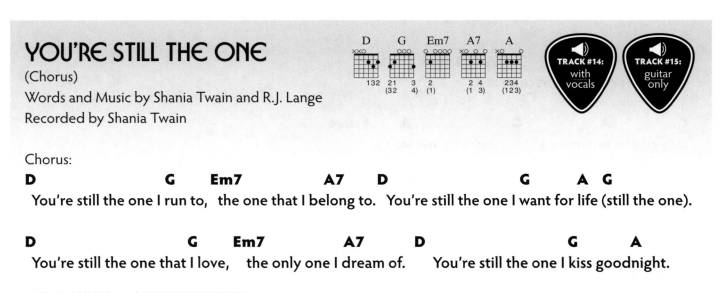

YOU'RE STILL THE ONE
(Chorus)
Words and Music by Shania Twain and R.J. Lange
Recorded by Shania Twain

Chorus:

D   G   Em7   A7   D   G   A   G
You're still the one I run to,   the one that I belong to.   You're still the one I want for life (still the one).

D   G   Em7   A7   D   G   A
You're still the one that I love,   the only one I dream of.   You're still the one I kiss goodnight.

Am7 CHORD

Another commonly used minor seventh chord is Am7. Because it's related to the A minor chord you learned earlier, its fingering is similar.

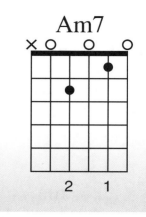

Am7

» Chord-Changing Tips

A few things to keep in mind while practicing the next song:

- ⊙ Check out the quick change from C to Am7. It's fast, but it's easy— just lift up your third finger, and your C chord instantly turns into an Am7!

- ⊙ Another quick change happens when you alternate from the D to the Dsus4 and back. This kind of change is super common in popular guitar songs.

- ⊙ The chord changes after the last line of the chorus can all be played in virtually the same hand position. Try this section using the four-fingered G major chord from page 22 and the alternative C major chord (Cadd9) shown below.

"Be different, stand out, and work your butt off."
~Reba McEntire

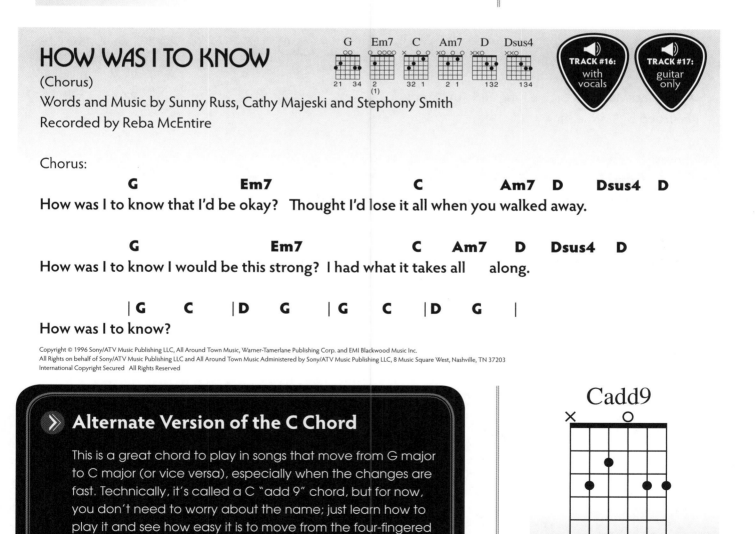

HOW WAS I TO KNOW
(Chorus)
Words and Music by Sunny Russ, Cathy Majeski and Stephony Smith
Recorded by Reba McEntire

Chorus:

       G   **Em7**   **C**   **Am7** **D**   **Dsus4** **D**
How was I to know that I'd be okay?   Thought I'd lose it all when you walked away.

       G   **Em7**   **C** **Am7**   **D**   **Dsus4** **D**
How was I to know I would be this strong? I had what it takes all   along.

        |**G**   **C** |**D** **G** |**G**   **C** |**D**   **G** |
How was I to know?

» Alternate Version of the C Chord

This is a great chord to play in songs that move from G major to C major (or vice versa), especially when the changes are fast. Technically, it's called a C "add 9" chord, but for now, you don't need to worry about the name; just learn how to play it and see how easy it is to move from the four-fingered G major chord to this cool C chord.

Cadd9

MAJOR SEVENTH CHORDS

Major seventh chords tend to have a bright, jazzy quality. They are absolute fixtures in jazz music and are also found in rock, country, and pop songs, as you'll see in the next tune. To get a feel for how the major seventh chord sounds in relation to its parent major chord, try alternating between the C chord (which you already know) and Cmaj7 (shown below). For this next song excerpt, you'll also need to know the Gmaj7 and F#5 chords:

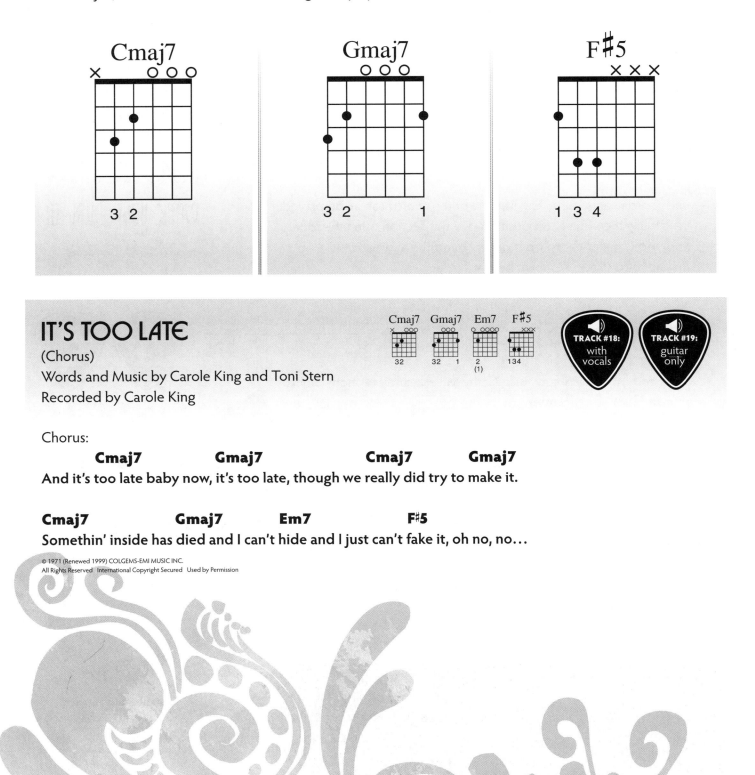

IT'S TOO LATE

(Chorus)

Words and Music by Carole King and Toni Stern

Recorded by Carole King

TRACK #18: with vocals
TRACK #19: guitar only

Chorus:

  Cmaj7   **Gmaj7**   **Cmaj7**   **Gmaj7**

And it's too late baby now, it's too late, though we really did try to make it.

Cmaj7   **Gmaj7**   **Em7**   **F#5**

Somethin' inside has died and I can't hide and I just can't fake it, oh no, no…

PASSING CHORDS: D/F♯

Passing chords, loosely defined, are "in-between" chords that help you get smoothly from one chord to another. A very special passing chord used in popular guitar songs is D/F♯ (pronounced "D over F-sharp"). This is the first time you'll be using your left thumb to fret a note. Curl your thumb around the neck so you can depress the 2nd fret of the low E string while you play your regular D chord. Now you don't have to avoid playing that sixth string because it's an important part of the chord!

D/F♯ is commonly used as a passing chord between E minor and G major. Notice that you hear a smooth, step-by-step bass line played on the low E string in each direction. Try playing this sequence yourself:

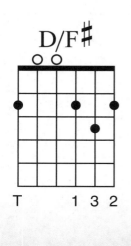

Em D/F♯ G D/F♯ Em

YOU'RE STILL THE ONE

(Verse)

Words and Music by Shania Twain and R.J. Lange
Recorded by Shania Twain

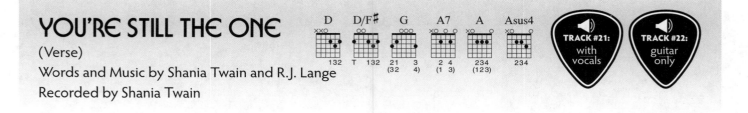

Verse:

D   D/F♯   G   A7
　　Looks like we made it; look how far we've come, my baby.

D   D/F♯   G   A7
　　We mighta took the long way;   we knew we'd get there someday.

D   D/F♯   G   A7   D   G   A   Asus4   A
　　They said   "I'll bet   they'll never make it," but just look at us holdin' on.

　　　　　D   G   A   G   D
We're still together, still goin' strong.   (You're still the one.)

CHAPTER FOUR:
COOL CHORD VOICINGS

ADDING SPARKLE

THIS NEXT section introduces you to some chords that are easy to execute and will open up your playing tremendously. Most guitar players don't learn these *voicings* (arrangements of notes within a chord) when they first start out, so you may fool people into thinking that you've been playing for far longer than you actually have been. Don't worry... it'll be our little secret!

SUPER-USEFUL CHORD: THE "ALTERNATIVE" Bm

B minor is usually played as a barre chord, which is a type of chord that can be very tough for beginners to master. Fortunately, you'll be learning an alternative version of the chord that is much easier to play, and it sounds fantastic. Technically, the chord you'll be playing is called B minor "add 11," but don't let the name scare you! It's actually easier to play than a plain-old B minor (and when you *do* learn how to play the B minor barre chord, you can interchange it with this version as you see fit).

Bm(add11)

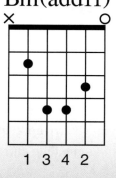

⟫ Chord Tip: Bm

When you play this chord, try muting the low E string with your left index finger. Touch the string lightly so it doesn't vibrate. That way, if your right hand accidentally strums the low E string, it won't make an ugly sound that doesn't belong in the chord.

E7 is another chord you'll need to know in order to play the next song.

E7

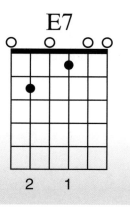

"I have been told by some people that I was the first woman they ever actually saw give a downbeat. Fine, cool." ~Carole King

IT'S TOO LATE
(Verse & Chorus)
Words and Music by Carole King and Toni Stern
Recorded by Carole King

Bm(add11) E7 Am7 Gmaj7 Cmaj7 F#5

TRACK #23: with vocals
TRACK #24: guitar only

Verse:

Bm(add11)   **E7**
Stayed in bed all mornin' just to pass the time.

Bm(add11)   **E7**
There's somethin' wrong here, there can be no denyin'.

Bm(add11)   **Am7**   **Gmaj7**
One of us is changin', or maybe we've just stopped tryin'.

Chorus:
         Cmaj7   **Gmaj7**   **Cmaj7**   **Gmaj7**
And it's too late baby now, it's too late, though we really did try to make it.

Cmaj7   **Gmaj7**   **Em7**   **F#5**   **Bm(add11)**
Somethin' inside has died and I can't hide and I just can't fake it, oh no…

 Practice Tip
When moving from the Bm(add11) chord to the Am7, simply lift your first finger, slide your other three fingers down to the 1st and 2nd frets (keeping them in position), lift your fourth finger, and you've arrived at Am7. When you get really good at this change, try lifting both your first and fourth fingers at the same time and *then* slide your fingers into position for the Am7.

C/D CHORD
The C/D chord (pronounced "C over D") is a moody, sophisticated-sounding chord that's often used in pop and jazz music. Here are two different fingerings for it; try both and see which you prefer. Make sure you don't play the low E string on either version (mute the string with your left hand, or avoid it with your right… or both).

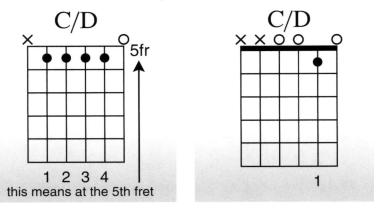

"I've watched my peers get better with age and hoped that would happen with me." ~Bonnie Raitt

LOVE SNEAKIN' UP ON YOU

(Chorus)

Words and Music by Jimmy Scott and Tom Snow
Recorded by Bonnie Raitt

C/D   Bm(add11)   C

TRACK #25: with vocals
TRACK #26: guitar only

Chorus:

C/D   **Bm(add11)**   **C**

Don't worry baby, ain't nothin' new; that's just love sneakin' up on you.

     C/D   **Bm(add11)**   **C**

If your whole world is shakin', baby, feel like I do, that's just love sneakin' up on you.

CHORD ALTERNATIVE: LET B & E RING!

Another great sound is to let your B and high E strings ring out. Try it when you play an alternative version of B7. A traditional open B7 is shown here as well as our alternative version with open B and E strings (which would technically be called B "7 add 11"). It's a lot easier to play when you've got quick chord changes going on, and a great option to use when you're first learning the next song.

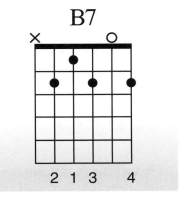

B7

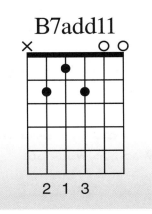

B7add11

"I just do what comes out and I don't fight it. I make sure I'm just doing the best I can." ~KT Tunstall

BLACK HORSE AND THE CHERRY TREE

(Verse)

Words and Music by Katie Tunstall
Recorded by KT Tunstall

Intro:

     Em   **B7add11** **Em**   **B7add11** **Em**
Woo-hoo, woo-hoo,   woo-hoo, woo-hoo.

Verse:

Well my heart knows me better than I know myself,
So I'm gonna let it do all the talking.

     Em   **B7add11**   **Em**
Woo-hoo, woo-hoo.

I came across a place in the middle of nowhere,
With a big black horse and a cherry tree.

     Em   **B7add11**   **Em**
Woo-hoo, woo-hoo.

I felt a little fear upon my back,
I said, "Don't look back, just keep on walking."

     Em   **B7add11**   **Em**
Woo-hoo, woo-hoo.

When the big black horse said, "Look this way,"
Said, "Hey, lady, will you marry me?"

     Em   **B7add11**   **Em**
Woo-hoo, woo-hoo.

MOVEABLE OPEN C CHORD

Try sliding your C chord up two frets to an open D chord (technically, D "add 2/4"). Mute the low E string with your left thumb for both chords. This version of a D chord is a bit moodier sounding than the more traditional fingering, which makes it perfect for the chorus of "Black Horse and the Cherry Tree." Try both versions and see which you prefer.

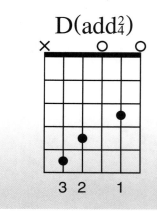

$D(add\frac{2}{4})$

BLACK HORSE AND THE CHERRY TREE

(Chorus)

Words and Music by Katie Tunstall

Recorded by KT Tunstall

Chorus:

　　　　　Em　Dadd2/4　　C

But I said no,　　no,　　no,　　no no no.

　　　　Em　Dadd2/4　　　C　　　　　　　　　Em

I said no,　　no,　　　　　you're not the one for me.

　　　　　　　D(add2/4)　　　　　C

No,　　no,　　no,　　no no no.

　　　　Em　Dadd2/4　C

I said no,　　no,　　　you're not the one for me.

MOVEABLE OPEN E CHORD

This is one of my favorite techniques. Take your basic E chord fingering and experiment by moving it all over the neck. To do this, you'll want to use the alternate fingering for your E chord (shown below), so your first finger is free to fret the low E string when you move the chord up the neck. Notice that when you move the open E chord around, you're also letting the B and high E strings ring open.

Try playing the chords below, and then, using the same finger positioning, move the open E chord to different places all over the neck. As you'll discover for yourself, at some positions it'll sound great; at others, not so much.

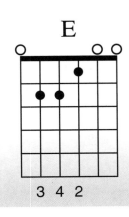

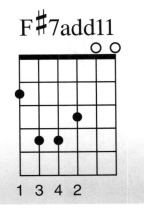

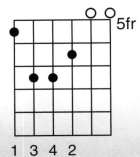

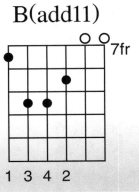

"I love songs that are very autobiographical." ~*Alanis Morissette*

YOU OUGHTA KNOW

(Chorus)

Lyrics by Alanis Morissette
Music by Alanis Morissette and Glen Ballard
Recorded by Alanis Morissette

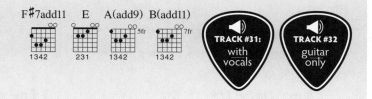

Chorus:

F#7add11   E   A(add9)   B(add11)
And I'm here   to remind you of the mess you left when you went away.

F#7add11   E   A(add9)   B(add11)
It's not fair   to deny me of the cross I bear that you gave to me. You, you, you oughta know.

"My older sister encouraged me from early on and bought me one of the first guitars I had. She listened to all of the crappy songs that I wrote when I was eight years old and encouraged me to keep doing it."
~ *Tracy Chapman*

Bad to the Bone

While you're learning any new skill, you're going to be pretty bad (sometimes painfully so) until you get good. This goes for both guitar playing *and* songwriting. Don't let that discourage you! Your first song will most likely *not* be your best. However, if you're going to write great songs, it's important to just start writing and to practice, practice, practice. Try not to judge your songs too much as you write. Just go with the flow while the ideas come to you. Later on, you can review your songs and re-write the parts that need improvement. (See more about songwriting in Chapter 8.)

5

CHAPTER FIVE:

POWER CHORDS

"Once I picked up an electric guitar, I lost interest in piano, and I just wanted to rock." *~Juliana Hatfield*

IT'S TIME TO ROCK OUT!

ALRIGHT, now, time to crank up your amp and rock out on your electric guitar! If you don't have an electric yet, you can go to your favorite guitar shop and practice your power chords through one of their guitars and amps. It's a good way to start familiarizing yourself with the many different kinds of electric guitars that are available—especially the differences in how they sound and feel—so when you're ready to buy yours, you can choose just the right one.

Of course, you can always play power chords on your acoustic guitar. It's just fun to have an extra excuse to turn up your amp and crank the distortion!

E-BASED POWER CHORDS

Power chords only contain two notes but are often fretted with three fingers (two fingers are playing the same note in different places). Power chords are notated with the suffix "5," and they're used in thousands and thousands of rock songs. The first type of power chord we'll check out is based along the low E string. Take care to only strum the lowest three strings and/or mute the top three strings by laying your first finger lightly across them.

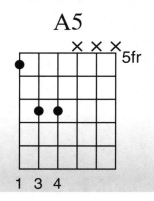

WE GOT THE BEAT

(Verse)

Words and Music by Charlotte Caffey
Recorded by The Go-Go's

Verse:

A5

See the people walkin' down the street, fall in line just watchin' all their feet.

They don't know where they want to go, but they're walkin' in time.

A-BASED POWER CHORDS

These power chords are shaped the same as the E-based power chords; they're just moved down one string to the A string. Let's learn some!

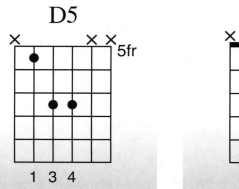

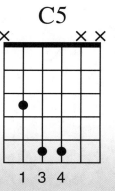

Use these E-based power chords in the next song as well:

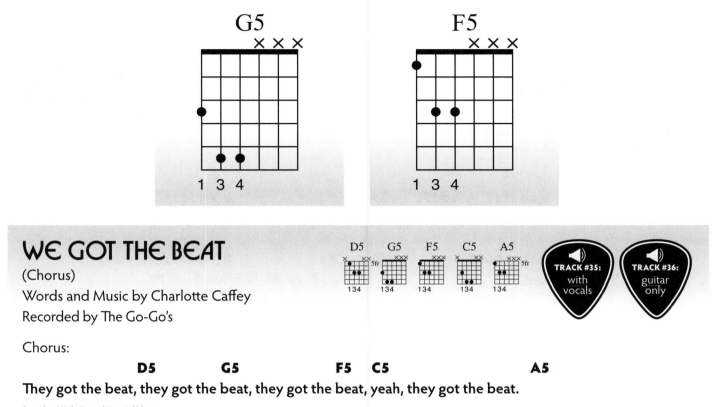

WE GOT THE BEAT

(Chorus)

Words and Music by Charlotte Caffey

Recorded by The Go-Go's

Chorus:

D5	**G5**	**F5**	**C5**	**A5**

They got the beat, they got the beat, they got the beat, yeah, they got the beat.

POWER CHORDS & OPEN CHORDS TOGETHER: MIXING IT UP

It can be fun to alternate between power chords and open chords within the same song. Try it on the next song, and use these new power chords:

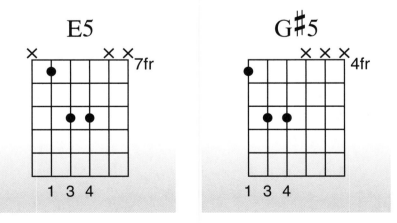

Song Notes: Soak Up the Sun

On the verses, try using the B(add11) and A(add9) chord alternatives you learned in Chapter 4 (under Moveable Open E Chords). Then try playing the E-based power chords B5 and A5. Both options work; it's just a matter of your personal preference.

On the chorus, try using your second, third, and fourth fingers for the initial E chord, so your first finger is free to fret the low E string of the B(add11) and A(add9) chords, as well as on the E-based power chords (F#5 and G#5).

"Music commands how we feel,
dictates what we experience in our feelings." ~Sheryl Crow

SOAK UP THE SUN

(Verse & Chorus)

E5 D5 B(add11) A(add9) E F#5 G#5

Words and Music by Jeff Trott and Sheryl Crow
Recorded by Sheryl Crow

Verse:

E5 D5 E5   **B(add11)   A(add9)**   **E5 D5 E5**   **B(add11)   A(add9)**
My friend the communist   holds meetings in his RV.

E5 D5 E5   **B(add11)   A(add9)**   **E5 D5 E5**   **B(add11) A(add9)**
I can't afford his gas,   so I'm stuck here watching TV.

E5 D5 E5   B(add11)   A(add9)

E5 D5 E5   **B(add11) A(add9)**   **E5 D5 E5**   **B(add11) A(add9)**
I don't have digital;   I don't have diddly squat.

E5 D5   E5   **B(add11) A(add9)**   **E5 D5 E5**   **B(add11)   A(add9)**
It's not having what you want;   it's wanting what you've got.

Chorus:

E   **B(add11)**   **F#5 G#5 A(add9)   B(add11)**
I'm gonna soak up the sun; I'm gonna tell everyone to   lighten   up.   I'm gonna tell 'em that

E   **B(add11)**   **F#5 G#5 A(add9)   B(add11)**
I've got no one to blame, but every time I feel lame I'm   lookin'   up.   I'm gonna soak up the sun.

E5 D5 E5   B(add11) A(add9)   **E5 D5 E5   B(add11) A(add9)**
I'm gonna soak up the sun.

ELECTRIC VS. ACOUSTIC GUITAR: COMPARE AND CONTRAST

"The idea was for me to bring more of the acoustic side in, for the band to have the duality of Led Zeppelin. Then I got to play big, loud electric guitar, too, which was fun." ~Nancy Wilson

If you have the opportunity to play a song on both the acoustic and the electric guitar, take advantage of it (or go to your local guitar shop to play the guitar you don't yet have). Check out how the various songs you've learned sound different on acoustic guitar than on electric guitar, and also compare the sounds of different settings on the amp you're using—no distortion (clean), mild distortion, mega-distortion, etc. If you're lucky enough to have access to guitar effect pedals (for use with your electric guitar and amplifier), plug them in and see how they affect your sound.

Try playing the following songs that you've already learned using your different tools and ask yourself the following questions (by the way, there are no "right" answers):

- ◉ "You Oughta Know" – Do you prefer acoustic or electric guitar?
- ◉ "Soak Up the Sun" – Do you prefer a clean sound from the amp or a distorted sound? How distorted?

CHAPTER SIX:
RIGHT-HAND TECHNIQUES

SO FAR we've talked a lot about what your left hand should be doing. Now it's time to focus on your right hand (or strumming/picking hand if you're a lefty) to make your playing more exciting.

UP-DOWN-UP-SLAP: A POPULAR STRUMMING PATTERN

Despite the funny name, this strumming pattern is used in lots of great songs. Just like it sounds, it involves an upstroke, a downstroke, an upstroke, and a slap. In this case, a slap refers to stopping the sound of the strings using your strumming hand. The easiest way to do this is to keep your hand in strumming position (with your fingers a bit curled), and use the palm of your hand and thumb to mute all six strings at once (not with your hand outstretched as if you're slapping someone's cheek—not that you would do that, of course). For these next two songs, use up-down-up-slap throughout.

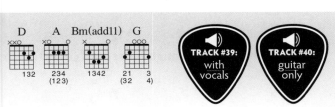

PROUD MARY

(Verse & Chorus)
Words and Music by John Fogerty
Recorded by Ike & Tina Turner

Verse:

D

Left a good job in the city, workin' for the man every night and day,

And I never lost one minute of sleepin', worryin' 'bout the way that things might've been.

Chorus:

A   **Bm(add11)**   **G**   **D**
Big wheel keep on turnin'; Proud Mary keep on burnin', and we're rollin', rollin', yeah rollin' on a river.

Alternative F#m Chord

For the next song, you'll need to know a new chord: F# minor. The traditional fingering of this chord is very tough to play. You'll learn it when you tackle barre chords, but for now, here's a fun alternative (technically called an F# minor "7 add 11," for those of you who want to show off to your guitar-playing buddies!).

"It's a marvelous feeling when someone says 'I want to do this song of yours' because they've connected to it. That's what I'm after." ~*Mary Chapin Carpenter*

GIRLS WITH GUITARS
(Verse)

Words and Music by Mary Chapin Carpenter
Recorded by Wynonna Judd

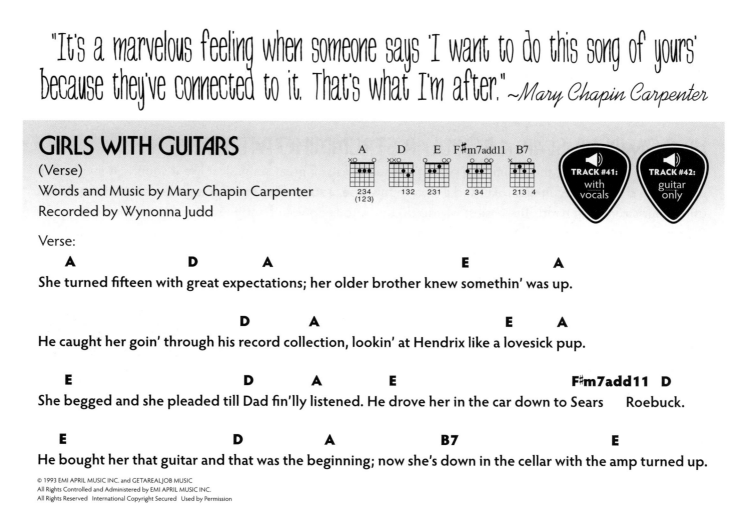

Verse:

   A   **D**   **A**   **E**   **A**

She turned fifteen with great expectations; her older brother knew somethin' was up.

             D   **A**   **E**   **A**

He caught her goin' through his record collection, lookin' at Hendrix like a lovesick pup.

  E   **D**   **A**   **E**   **F#m7add11** **D**

She begged and she pleaded till Dad fin'lly listened. He drove her in the car down to Sears   Roebuck.

  E   **D**   **A**   **B7**   **E**

He bought her that guitar and that was the beginning; now she's down in the cellar with the amp turned up.

PICKING SINGLE STRINGS

Sometimes, simply adding one note played on a single string can really spice up a song. Check out the following signature guitar riff that incorporates the slap you just learned, a single-string note, and some new power chords. The predominant strumming pattern used in this song is down-down-slap.

Note that the single-string note will be shown in the music in **_bold italics_**. It's a G note, which will be played by your second finger on the 3rd fret of the low E string. Once you're used to playing this riff, try *bending* that single note with your left hand (slightly pull the string toward the floor while holding the note) after the initial pitch rings out, and you'll sound *just* like the recording!

First, try out these new power chords. Here, the E5 and A5 are both *open* power chords, where the bass notes are played with the open E and A strings, respectively, instead of fretted like the moveable versions you learned earlier.

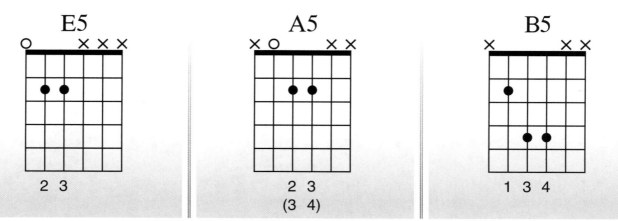

"My guitar is not a thing. It is an extension of myself. It is who I am." ~Joan Jett

I LOVE ROCK 'N ROLL

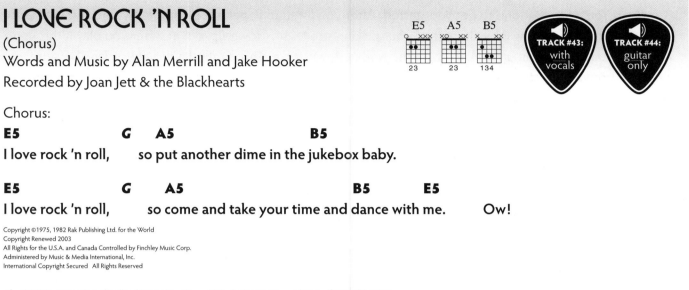

(Chorus)

Words and Music by Alan Merrill and Jake Hooker

Recorded by Joan Jett & the Blackhearts

Chorus:

E5		**G**	**A5**		**B5**	
I love rock 'n roll,			so put another dime in the jukebox baby.			

E5		**G**	**A5**		**B5**	**E5**	
I love rock 'n roll,			so come and take your time and dance with me.			Ow!	

FAST STRUMMING & CHORD CHANGES

The next song will help you practice changing chords while you're doing some fast strumming. At the end of the verse, there's a break to the fast strumming where you can try out a new chord: D/E (it's fingered just like C/D, only two frets higher). This tune also features the new Dm chord.

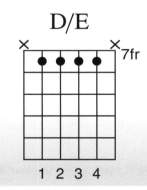

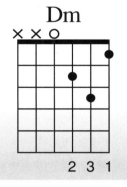

CRAZY ON YOU

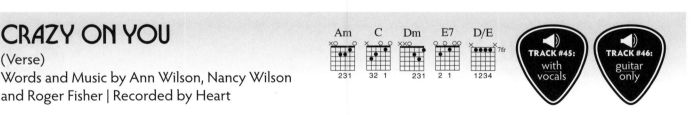

(Verse)

Words and Music by Ann Wilson, Nancy Wilson
and Roger Fisher | Recorded by Heart

Verse:

	Am		**C**	**Dm**		**E7**
We may still have time, we might still get by. Every time I think about it, I wanna cry.						

	Am		**C**	**Dm**	
With bombs and the devils and the kids keep comin', nowhere to breathe easy.					

E7

No time to be young.

Am	**D/E**		**Am**	**D/E**

SINGLE-STRING RIFFS & ALTERNATE PICKING

One of the really fun things about playing the guitar is all the cool riffs you get to play! The main riff from "Crazy on You" is a great one to get you started. After you listen to it, get a feel for the rhythm, and familiarize yourself with it, try playing it by alternating your picking strokes up-down-up-down. After you play it through a few times starting with an upstroke, try starting with a downstroke. This is called *alternate picking* because you alternate between upstrokes and downstrokes, and it's a good technique to practice. But first, you'll need to learn how to read tablature. Don't worry—it's easy!

Intro to Tablature

Tablature ("tab" for short) is a great way to notate guitar music. Tab tells you exactly where to place your fingers on the fretboard, and in what order. The easiest way to think about tab is a visual snapshot of your guitar fretboard, but without the frets. Try this: lay your guitar face up on a table, with the headstock to your left. Look down at the fretboard and then look at the sample tab below—see how the tab looks a lot like your guitar neck?

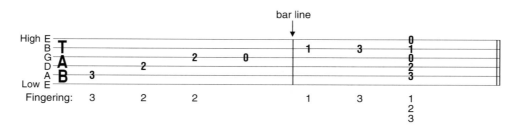

- The six horizontal lines represent the strings of the guitar. The top line represents the high E string, the bottom line represents the low E string, and the other lines are the strings in between.

- The numbers written on the lines show you which fret to play on which string. The number "0" represents an open string—just play the string without fretting it.

- Numbers stacked on top of each other are played simultaneously (i.e., strummed like a chord).

- In this book, left-hand fingerings are notated under the tab staff. This way you know which fingers to use to fret the notes. 1=index, 2=middle, 3=ring, and 4=pinky. Don't be surprised if you find tab elsewhere that doesn't include left-hand fingerings; it's an optional feature.

- The vertical line has nothing to do with the guitar's fretboard. It represents the bar line, which divides measures (a way of keeping time) in conventional music notation.

CRAZY ON YOU

(Riff)
Words and Music by Ann Wilson, Nancy Wilson and Roger Fisher
Recorded by Heart

TRACK #47: guitar only

```
T|------------------------------|------------------------------|------------------------------|----------------|
A|--2---0-----------------------|------------------------------|----2---0---------------------|----------------|
B|0---------3--2--0-------------|-----------------3------------|0---------3--2--0-------------|--------------3-|
                        1                                                          1
Fingering:  1     2  1     1              2           1     2  1     1              2
```

```
|------------------------------|------------------------------|------------------------------|-----------|
|----2---0---------------------|----2---0---------------------|----2---0---------------------|-----------|
|0---------3--2--0-------------|0---------3--2--0-------------|0---------3--2----------------|0----------|
                        3                                1                        3
        1     2  1        2              1     2  1     1              1     2  1     2
```

PALM MUTING

Palm muting is a technique in which the heel of your right hand lays lightly on the strings, right in front of the bridge (see picture). This deadens (or mutes) the sound of the strings, typically giving your note or chord a heavier sound. Try using palm muting when you play power chords, and use it in the next song. Before you play it, check out this new power chord:

C#5

Song Notes: Give Me One Reason
To spice up this song (and to make it sound more like Tracy Chapman's recording), try playing an open low E string before your F# chord. It's a fun variation, and while Tracy doesn't do it every time she plays the F#, she does use it a lot! Once you've got that down, try playing the open A string before your B5 for another cool variation on the recording.

GIVE ME ONE REASON

(Chorus)
Words and Music by Tracy Chapman
Recorded by Tracy Chapman

F#5   B5   C#5

TRACK #48: with vocals   **TRACK #49:** guitar only

Chorus:

F#5   **B5**   **C#5**   **F#5**
Give me one reason to stay here   and I'll turn right back around.

B5   **C#5**   **F#5**
Give me one reason to stay here and I'll turn right back around.

   C#5   **B5**   **F#5**
Said I don't wanna leave you lonely,   you've gotta make me change my mind.

ALL POWER CHORDS, ALL PALM MUTED

Now that you've tried some palm muting, let's go back to "Soak Up the Sun" and try palm muting all of the verse chords. So this time, instead of playing the moveable open E versions of the B and A chords in the verses, play E-based B5 and A5 chords (i.e., power chords), and keep them muted with your palm. Notice how the chorus really opens up when you finally get to strum those open chorus chords.

"There's a lot of integrity with musicians; you really still aspire to grow, and be great, to be the best version of yourself you can be." ~*Sheryl Crow*

SOAK UP THE SUN
(Verse & Chorus)
Words and Music by Jeff Trott and Sheryl Crow
Recorded by Sheryl Crow

E5   D5   B5   A5   E

B(add11)   F#5   G#5   A(add9)

TRACK #50: with vocals

TRACK #51: guitar only

Verse:

E5 D5 E5   **B5   A5**   **E5 D5 E5**   **B5   A5**
　　　　My friend the communist　　　　　　holds meetings in his RV.

E5 D5 E5   **B5   A5**   **E5 D5 E5**   **B5   A5**
　　　　I can't afford his gas,　　　　　　so I'm stuck here watching TV.

|E5   D5   E5   **B5|**   **A5**   **|**

E5 D5 E5   **B5 A5**   **E5 D5 E5**   **B5   A5**
　　　　I don't have digital,　　　　　　I don't have diddly squat.

E5 D5 E5   **B5   A5** **E5 D5 E5**   **B5   A5**
　　　　It's not having what you want,　　　　it's wanting what you've got.

Chorus:

E   **B(add11)**   **F#5 G#5 A(add9) B(add11)**
I'm gonna soak up the sun; I'm gonna tell everyone to   lighten   up.   I'm gonna tell 'em that

E   **B(add11)**   **F#5   G#5   A(add9)   B(add11)**
I've got no one to blame, but every time I feel lame I'm   lookin'   up.   I'm gonna soak up the sun.

E5 D5 E5   B5   **A5**   **E5 D5 E5**   **B5   A5**
　　　　I'm gonna soak up the sun.

CHUNK-A-CHUNK: A POWERFUL RHYTHMIC COMPONENT

So, you've tried muting strings with your left hand while your right hand aims to avoid the string in question (e.g., the low E string in B minor), and you've tried muting strings with your right hand while you fret them with your left hand (i.e., palm muting). Q: Well, what happens when you purposely strum a string that you're muting with your left hand? A: You get a really funky sound that I like to refer to as "chunk-a-chunk." Try it by lightly laying your left hand across the strings around the 5th fret; don't press down hard enough to hear any notes, but just hard enough to dampen the sound. Now strum the guitar with firm upstrokes and downstrokes. You should hear a sound similar to the example on Track 52.

Now it's time to try incorporating the chunk-a-chunk into a song. Try palm muting the chords during the verses, and use the chunk-a-chunk in the "Cake!" breaks. Listen to the recording, and you'll hear what I mean.

BIRTHDAY BOOGALOO

Words and Music by Ali Handal and Ernie Halter
Recorded by Ali Handal

A   E   A
Happy Birthday to you, Birthday Boogaloo. It's your own special day, eat a whole birthday cake.

D   A   E   D   A
Dance, scream, and shout, and blow the candles out. Happy Birthday to you, do the Birthday Boogaloo.

A   *chunk-a-chunk*   A   *chunk-a-chunk*   A   *chunk-a-chunk*   A
Cake!   Cake!   Cake!   Cake!

A   E   A
Happy Birthday to you, Birthday Boogaloo. When no one's watching you, you can do it in your birthday suit.

D   A   E   D   A
Stand up and cheer, it only comes once a year. Happy Birthday to you, Birthday Boogaloo.

A   *chunk-a-chunk*   A   *chunk-a-chunk*   A   *chunk-a-chunk*   A
Cake!   Cake!   Cake!   Cake!

D   A   E   D   A
Stand up and cheer, it only comes once a year. Happy Birthday to you, Birthday Boogaloo.

A   *chunk-a-chunk*   A   *chunk-a-chunk*   A   *chunk-a-chunk*   A
Cake!   Cake!   Cake!   Cake!

FINGERPICKING (A.K.A. FINGERSTYLE)

Fingerpicking (or *fingerstyle*) is when you pluck the strings with your thumb and fingers, instead of using a guitar pick. A very common fingerstyle technique involves picking down on the lower strings with your thumb, and picking up on the higher strings with your first, second, and third fingers.

The photo shows a good hand position for fingerstyle. Place your hand over the sound hole and keep a slight arch to the wrist. The thumb plucks down on the strings at a slight angle, and the fingers pluck upward.

Try this simple exercise to get the feel of fingerpicking: start by placing your first, second, and third fingers under the G, B, and high E strings, respectively. Keeping your fingers in that position, individually pick down on the low E, A, and D strings with your thumb. As you do so, let your thumb come to rest momentarily on the adjacent string.

Next play the top three strings: pluck up on the G string with your first finger, up on the B string with your second finger, and up on the high E string with your third finger. Do your best to keep the volume of all of the notes consistent by applying the same amount of plucking pressure.

In this next song, you'll be practicing your fingerpicking with a new chord: G/B (pronounced "G over B"). The fingers of your right hand will be assigned to the following strings: your thumb will pluck the A string, your first finger will pluck the D string, your second finger will pluck the G string, and your third finger will pluck the B string.

For the next song, listen to the recording to hear how it's supposed to sound, and remember to practice the fingerpicking *slowly* until you get the hang of it. It's always better to practice a technically challenging part slowly until you can play it without any mistakes. Once you've got the part down at a slow tempo, it's much easier to speed up until you're playing it perfectly *and* at the right tempo.

G/B

LANDSLIDE

(Picking Pattern)
Words and Music by Stevie Nicks
Recorded by Fleetwood Mac

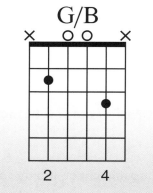

TRACK #55:
guitar
only

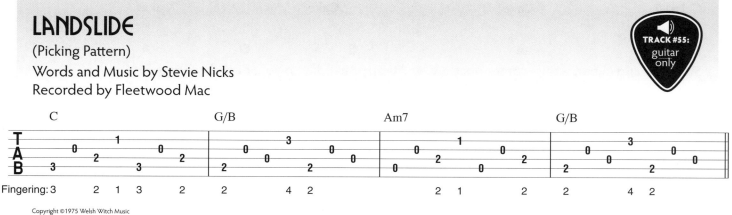

7

CHAPTER SEVEN:

FUN STUFF

CAPOS: THEIR USE AND ABUSE

THE *CAPO* is a wonderful invention that allows you to play open-position chords in any key. It's a small device that you can temporarily clamp to the neck of the guitar, and it presses down on all of the strings wherever you place it. This shortens the length of the strings, which effectively creates a new nut. For example, if you attach the capo to the 1st fret, all of the strings sound a *half step* (one fret) higher in pitch. So if you then play an E chord, it will *sound* like an F chord.

This is fantastic if the song you want to play is a bit too low for you to sing (or a singer you're accompanying). If you don't want to learn a whole bunch of new chords in order to play the song in a higher key, you can simply use a capo to raise the key on the guitar and play the song as you normally would. With your capo, you can play a song in any key, using the same open-chord voicings you've already learned.

So, how does one "abuse" a capo? Occasionally (alright, more than occasionally), beginner guitarists rely too heavily on their capos. After learning a total of four or five chords, they proceed to play every song they can with only those chords, and simply use a capo to change the key of the song they're playing. This is a lazy way to play guitar and is usually *very* boring for your audience. Used sparingly, a capo is a miraculous tool that can help you play many songs, but when it's over-used in place of learning new chords in new positions, it can easily become a crutch and a hindrance to improvement.

That being said, let's use the capo in the way it was intended. Remember the fingerpicking progression you learned for "Landslide?" Well, you learned it in the key of G (starting on a C chord), but the Fleetwood Mac recording is actually in the key of Bb. The key of G might have been too low for Stevie Nicks to sing, but she sounds fantastic in the key of Bb. Let's try playing the song with your capo on the 3rd fret so she can sing with you (and if Stevie's not there, you can sing with you!).

Capo Tip
The chords indicated in the song reflect the chord shapes to use—not the actual sounds produced by making those shapes. The actual chords produced will be three half steps higher than the chord shapes fretted, because you've put your capo on the 3rd fret of the guitar.

"I love haunting, haunted melodies." ~Stevie Nicks

LANDSLIDE

(Verse)

Words and Music by Stevie Nicks

Recorded by Fleetwood Mac

(See page 50 for the "Landslide" fingerpicking pattern. Use capo at the 3rd fret.)

C   G/B   Am7

TRACK #56: with vocals

TRACK #57: guitar only

Capo 3

Intro:

C   G/B   Am7   G/B

Verse:

C   G/B   Am7   G/B   C   G/B   Am7   G/B
   I took my love, took it down.   I climbed a mountain and I turned around.

     C   G/B   Am7   G/B   C   G/B   Am7   G/B
And I saw my reflection in the snow-covered hills,   till the landslide brought it down.

     C   G/B   Am7   G/B   C   G/B   Am7   G/B
Oh, mirror in the sky, what is love?   Can the child within my heart rise above?

      C   G/B   Am7 G/B   C   G/B   Am7 G/B
Can I sail through the changin' ocean tides? Can I handle the seasons of my life?

C   G/B   Am7   G/B   C

Other Capo Uses

Sometimes, when an artist writes and performs a song on another instrument (e.g., piano), the chords don't translate very easily to the guitar. This is another instance where a capo can be helpful. This next song has been made much easier to play by changing the key of the song to a more "guitar-friendly" key (from C♯ to G). Then we use a capo at the 6th fret to bring the song back to its original key (C♯), while playing the chords from the easier key (G). (Sound confusing? It won't be, once you study music theory!) Feel free to experiment with fingerpicking, strumming, or both in this song.

First, you'll need to know these new chords:

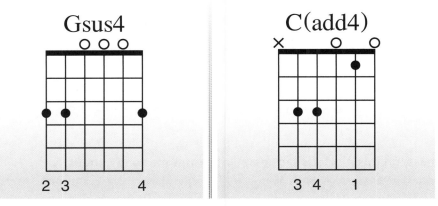

"I sort of feel like music saved my life when I was young. This is the one thing that I knew I was good at." ~Sarah McLachlan

ANGEL

Words and Music by Sarah McLachlan
Recorded by Sarah McLachlan

G   Gsus4   Am   C
D   Bm(add11)   C(add4)

TRACK #58: with vocals

TRACK #59: guitar only

Capo 6
Intro:

G   Gsus4   G   Gsus4

Verse:

                  Am   **C**   **G**   **D**
Spend all your time waitin' for that second chance, for a break that would make it ok.

                  Am   **C**   **G**   **D**
There's always some reason to feel not good enough, and it's hard at the end of the day.

             Am   **C**   **G**   **D**
I need some distraction, oh beautiful release, memories seep from my veins.

            Am   **C**   **G**   **D**
Let me be empty, oh and weightless, and maybe I'll find some peace tonight.

Chorus:

  G   **Gsus4** **G**   **Bm(add11)**
In the arms of the   angel, fly away from here

        C **C(add4)**   **C**   **C(add4)** **C**   **G**   **D**
From this dark, cold   hotel room   and the endlessness that you fear.

     G   **C**   **G**   **Bm(add11)**   **C** **C(add4)** **C** **C(add4)** **C**
You are pulled from the wreckage of your silent reverie; you're in the arms of the   angel.

     G   **D**   **G**   **C**   **G**   **Gsus4**
May you find   some comfort here.

Verse:

                Am   **C**   **G**   **D**
So tired of the straight line and ev'rywhere you turn there's vultures and thieves at your back.

               Am   **C**   **G**   **D**
Storm keeps on twistin', keep on buildin' the lies that you make up for all that you lack.

               Am   **C**   **G**   **D**
It don't make no   difference, escaping one last time; it's easier to believe

              Am   **C**   **G**   **D**
In this sweet madness, oh this glorious sadness, that brings me to my knees.

Chorus:

    G   Gsus4 G   Bm(add11)

In the arms of the angel, fly away from here

         C   C(add4)   C   C(add4) C   G   D

From this dark, cold   hotel room   and the endlessness that you fear.

         G Gsus4 G   Gsus4   G   Bm(add11)   C   C(add4)   C

You are pulled from the wreckage of your silent reverie; you're in the arms of the   angel.

         G   D   G   C   C(add4) C   C(add4) C

May you find   some comfort here. You're in the arms of the   angel.

         G   D   G   C   G   C   G   C   G

May you find   some comfort here.

ALTERNATE TUNINGS

"When you tune your guitar in a different way, it lends itself to a new way of looking at your songwriting." ~Sheryl Crow

For some artists, new tunings inspire fresh musical ideas, so they deviate from *standard tuning* (the tuning we've been using so far). There are many ways you can choose to tune your guitar, and many great songs utilize alternate tunings.

DROP D TUNING

Drop D is one of the simplest alternate tunings. From *standard tuning*, simply tune your sixth string (normally the low E string) down one full step to D. It'll sound similar to your fourth string, just an *octave* lower (to use music theory terminology). Note that an electronic tuner (in particular, a *chromatic* tuner) is very useful for tuning your guitar to different tunings.

TRACK #60: Drop D Tuning Notes

Use Track 60 drop your low E string down for Drop D tuning:

In Drop D tuning, you can play power chords by simply barring your first finger across the lowest three strings and strumming (don't strum the highest three strings, and/or take care to mute them with your left hand). Try playing Joan Jett's "I Love Rock 'N Roll" riff in Drop D tuning, in the key of D. Check out the tab below.

I LOVE ROCK 'N ROLL

(Chorus)
Words and Music by Alan Merrill and Jake Hooker

TRACK #61: guitar only

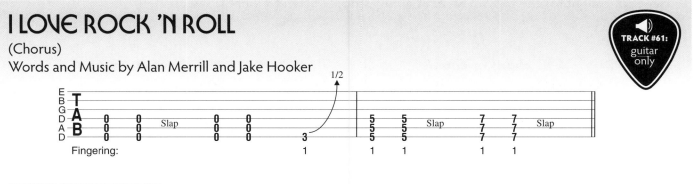

PUTTING IT ALL TOGETHER

This next tune features many of the techniques you've learned so far: Drop D tuning, power chords, chunk-a-chunk, and palm muting. Listen to the recorded example several times to hear where each musical element comes into play—where are the power chords, which chords are muted, where are the slaps versus chunk-a-chunks? When you're ready to try it yourself, take it slowly and play small sections at a time.

In this song, you'll be using all Drop D power chords. You'll play the same shape all over the neck; just change which fret you play at, indicated by the numbers over the lyrics. When you see the number "0," play the lowest three strings open. In this example, the top three strings are never played. Here's a chord diagram for the power-chord shape you'll use throughout the tune (this one is F5, labeled as "3" above the lyrics).

F5
Power Chord in
Drop D Tuning

>> **Drop D Tip**
When playing the low D5 chord, it's especially important to use your left hand to mute the highest three strings so they don't ring out.

ALL THE WAY
(Verse & Chorus)
Words and Music by Ali Handal
Recorded by Ali Handal

TRACK #62: with vocals   TRACK #63: guitar only

Verse:

0   **[slap]**   **0**   **3**   **0**   **[slap]**   **0**   **5**
Guitar slingin' my soul starts singin', I'm back with my boys in the band.

   0   **[slap]** **0**   **3**   **0** **[slap]** **0**   **5**
Gonna rock you right, stay all night,   your wish, our command.

      0   **[slap]** **0**   **3**   **0**   **[slap]**   **0**   **5**
Comin' up through the clubs, feelin' the love   everybody keeps sendin' our way.

     0   **[slap]**   **0**   **3**   **0 10 0 10 0 10**
Headed straight for the top, no we ain't gonna stop;   listen to what I say.

Chorus:

         5   *chunk-a-chunk*   **10 5**   *chunk-a-chunk*   **10**
We're gonna go all the way (we're gonna go, we're gonna go).   All the way.

5   *chunk-a-chunk*   **10 5**   *chunk-a-chunk*   **10**
All the way (we're gonna go, we're gonna go).   All the way.   All the way.

0   **[slap]**   **3**   **0**   **[slap]**   **5**   **0**   **[slap]**   **3**   **0**   **[slap]**   **5**   **0**

ANOTHER ALTERNATE TUNING: EBBGBD

"It's interesting, because since the beginning, since I started writing little poems, of course my identity as a woman has informed my writing. Everything from how I perceive the world to the experiences I have, to, I think the way I play the guitar." ~Ani DiFranco

One of the fun things about some alternate tunings is that you can create all kinds of new sounds by simply moving one shape around the guitar neck, as Ani DiFranco does in this next song. In EBBGBD tuning, you're moving your highest (first) string down a whole step (from E to D), your fourth string down one and a half steps (from D to B), and your fifth string up one step (from A to B). Fortunately, the tuning is pretty much the hardest part about this next song!

Use Track 64 to match your guitar's strings to EBBGBD tuning:

TRACK #64: EBBGBD Tuning Notes

» Song Tip: Ani's Chord

For the next song, use a capo at the 2nd fret. Instead of writing the chord name above the lyrics, we've indicated the fret number above the capo where your second finger will be fretting the sixth (lowest) string of the chord shape. In the case of a "3," your second finger will be three frets above the capo (on the 5th fret, since the capo is on the 2nd fret). In the case of a "0," simply strum all of the open strings with no fretted notes at all; in this tuning, an open strum sounds beautifully haunting (technically, it's a different voicing of an Em7 chord, although it will sound like F#m7 because of the capo).

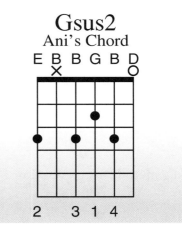

Gsus2
Ani's Chord

NOT A PRETTY GIRL

Words and Music by Ani DiFranco
Recorded by Ani DiFranco

Capo 2

Intro: 0   3   8   10   0   3   8   10

Verse:

          0   3 8   10   0   3   8   10

I am not a pretty girl,   that is not what I   do. I ain't no damsel in distress and I don't need to be rescued.

            0   3   8   10   5   8

So, so put me down punk, wouldn't you prefer a maiden fair, isn't there a kitten stuck up a tree somewhere?

  0   3   8   10

I am not an angry girl,   but it seems like I've got everyone fooled.

     0   3   8   10

Every time I say something they find hard to hear, they chalk it up to my anger and never to their own fear.

 0   3   8   10   0   3 8 10

Imagine you're a girl just trying to finally come clean, knowing full well they prefer you were dirty and smiling.

   0   3   8   10   5   8

And I am sorry   but I am not a maiden fair and I am not a kitten stuck up a tree somewhere.

Break: 0   3   8   10   0   3   8   10
          Ah,   hey,   ah.

Verse:

    0   3   8   10

And generally my generation   wouldn't be caught dead   working for the man.

   0   3   8   10

And generally I agree with them,   trouble is you got to have yourself an alternate plan and

0   3   8   10

I have earned my disillusionment.   I have been working all of my life.

  0 3   8   10

And I am a patriot,   I have been fighting the good fight,

    0   3   8   10

And what if there are no damsels in distress? What if I knew that and I called your bluff.

   5   8

Don't you think every kitten figures out how to get down, whether or not you ever show up?

0	3		8	10			0		3		8	10

Oh,   I   am not a pretty girl.   Oh,

| | | 0 | | 3 | | 8 | 10 |

I   don't really want to be a pretty girl.   Oh,

| | | 0 | | 3 | | 8 10 |

I   want to be more   than a pretty girl.   Hey,   ah.

Outro: **0**   **3**   **8 10 0**   **3**   **8**   **10**

Hey,   ah,   hey,   ah.   (*freely*)

SINGING WHILE PLAYING: TIPS & PRACTICE

Singing while playing the guitar comes easier for some than for others, but it is a skill that can be learned and improved. The most important things to remember are to take it slowly, break down what you're doing into small parts, and have lots of patience with yourself.

Take "We Got the Beat," for example. The verse is just one chord, so get used to playing that A5 in a straight up-and-down strumming rhythm. Then, once you've got that going, you can concentrate on singing. Your vocal rhythm may not be perfect at first, but just keep working on it.

For the chorus, the first thing to accomplish is to arrive at each chord on time. Initially, try singing the chorus without playing the guitar at all. Next, sing the chorus while strumming each chord just once when it first comes in. After you're comfortable with that, you can start filling in the guitar rhythm between chord changes. Visit www.AliHandal.com/Lessons to see a video example of this process.

A second approach is to completely master the guitar part first, and then add the vocal. Experiment with both approaches and see which works best for you.

WE GOT THE BEAT

(Verse and Chorus)

Words and Music by Charlotte Caffey
Recorded by The Go-Go's

Verse:
A5
See the people walkin' down the street, fall in line just watchin' all their feet.

They don't know where they want to go, but they're walkin' in time.

Chorus:
          D5   **G5**   **F5 C5**   **A5**
They got the beat, they got the beat, they got the beat, yeah, they got the beat.

For this next song, try using both learning approaches that you used on the chorus of "We Got the Beat." Sometimes, one method works well for one song, but not as well for another, so it's nice to have options. There are also some new chords to check out.

"Everybody has that point in their life where you hit a crossroads and you've had a bunch of bad days and there's different ways you can deal with it, and the way I dealt with it was I just turned completely to music." ~ *Taylor Swift*

MEAN

Words and Music by Taylor Swift
Recorded by Taylor Swift

Verse:

| C#m | Bsus4 | | Asus2 |
You, with your words like knives and swords and weapons that you use against me.

| C#m | Bsus4 | | Asus2 |
You have knocked me off my feet again, got me feeling like I'm nothing.

| C#m | Bsus4 | | Asus2 |
You, with your voice like nails on a chalkboard, calling me out when I'm wounded.

| C#m | Bsus4 | | Asus2 |
You,   pickin' on the weaker man.

Bsus4   E   Asus2 Bsus4   Asus2
        Well, you can take me down   with just one single   blow, but you don't know what you don't know.

Chorus:

E   Bsus4 C#m   Asus2 E   Bsus4   Asus2
Someday I'll be living in a big old city, and all you're ever gonna be is mean.

E   Bsus4 C#m   Asus2   E   Bsus4   Asus2
Someday I'll be   big enough so you can't hit me, and all you're ever gonna be is mean.

Asus2   E   D$_9^6$ – E5
Why you gotta be so mean?

Verse:

C#m   Bsus4   Asus2
You, with your switching sides and your wildfire lies and your humiliation.

C#m   Bsus4   Asus2
You have pointed out my flaws again as if I don't already see them.

```
C#m        Bsus4                      Asus2
```
I walk with my head down trying to block you out 'cause I never impress you.

```
C#m  Bsus4    Asus2
```
I just wanna feel ok again.

```
Bsus4                        E         Asus2      Bsus4
```
I'll bet you got pushed around,   somebody made you cold,   but the cycle ends right now,

```
        Asus2
```
'cause you can't lead me down that road and you don't know what you don't know.

Chorus:
```
E        Bsus4  C#m            Asus2  E      Bsus4        Asus2
```
Someday I'll be   living in a big old city, and all you're ever gonna be is mean.

```
E        Bsus4  C#m                  Asus2    E      Bsus4        Asus2
```
Someday I'll be   big enough so you can't hit me, and all you're ever gonna be is mean.

```
                      E        D#6 – E5   Bsus4   Asus2   Bsus4   Asus2
```
Why you gotta be so mean?

Bridge:
```
        Bsus4                      E         Asus2
```
And I can see you years from now in a bar   talking over a football game.

```
Bsus4                              E         Asus2
```
    With that same big loud opinion, but   nobody's listening.

```
Bsus4                          C#m     Bsus4 Asus2
```
    Washed up and ranting about the same old bitter   things.

```
Bsus4                        C#m     Bsus4 Asus2            E      Bsus4 C#m
```
Drunk and grumbling on about how I   can't   sing,   but all you are is mean.

```
Asus2    E        Bsus4 C#m        Asus2     E      Bsus4    C#m      Asus2
```
All you are is mean and a liar and pathetic and alone in life and mean, and mean, and mean, and mean.

Chorus:
(A'capella) *chunk-a-chunk*
But someday I'll be living in a big old city and all you're ever gonna be is mean. Yeah!

```
E        Bsus4  C#m            Asus2    E      Bsus4        Asus2
```
Someday I'll be big enough so you can't hit me and all you're ever gonna be is mean.

```
E        Bsus4  C#m            Asus2  E      Bsus4      Asus2
```
Someday I'll be   living in a big old city and all you're ever gonna be is mean.

```
E        Bsus4  C#m            Asus2    E      Bsus4        Asus2
```
Someday I'll be   big enough so you can't hit me and all you're ever gonna be is mean.

```
Asus2            E
```
Why you gotta be so mean?

CHAPTER EIGHT:

BEGINNING SONGWRITING TIPS

"When it's time to write a song, it's time to write it." ~Linda Perry

GET CREATIVE! JUST DO IT!

THERE are so many ways to begin writing a song, and there's no wrong way. Some people write alone, while others like to collaborate with a friend or a writing partner. Some songs start with a guitar chord, a whole chord progression, or just a single-string riff. Sometimes a song starts with a vocal melody or a lyric idea and the guitar part gets written later. The point is, there are lots of ways to express yourself with your guitar. The most important thing is to experiment and see what you come up with! I suggest that you play with ideas and techniques you've already learned as you experiment with writing your own music. Play around with the following:

- ⊙ **Moveable chord shapes (like the moveable open E chord)**
- ⊙ **Power chords**
- ⊙ **Single-note riffs/melodies**
- ⊙ **Alternate tunings** – feel free to make up your own! Just remember to write your new tuning down or record it afterwards, so you can return to it again. Or, use some of the open tunings that others have used; you can find a list of useful alternate tunings at www.AliHandal.com/Lessons.

SONGWRITERS VS. PERFORMERS

"I'm a songwriter first." ~Carole King

Lots of artists have #1 hits with songs that they didn't write. Other artists *only* record songs that they've written (or co-written) themselves. Most artists fit somewhere in between, writing their own songs and performing other songs that they didn't write, but enjoy performing.

The song "Landslide" that you learned in Chapter 6 was written by Stevie Nicks while she was a member of the rock band Fleetwood Mac. Fleetwood Mac had a hit with "Landslide" back in 1975. In 2002, over 25 years later, the Dixie Chicks recorded a country version of the song, which became a hit for them too. A great song is a great song.

Carole King started off as a songwriter, penning songs that were covered by countless other artists, including Aretha Franklin, James Taylor, and even the Beatles. Many years into her career as a songwriter, she released her own album as an artist, *Tapestry*, which went on to sell over 25 million copies, making her a superstar performing songwriter in her own right.

"I would encourage everybody to be as quirky as he or she wants to be. If you start writing songs thinking about what a hit is, you might as well just end your career right now." ~Linda Perry

On the opposite end of the spectrum, some women start off as rock stars and then become better known for their songwriting prowess. A great example is Linda Perry, who was known early in her career as a singer and member of the band 4 Non Blondes. Today she's known as a top songwriter and producer who has written and co-written countless hits with numerous artists. One of her best-known songs is "Beautiful," featured on the next page, which Christina Aguilera made an international hit in 2002. I hope you enjoy learning this expertly crafted, emotional song.

⟫ Chord Tips

Experiment with interchanging Dsus2 with a regular D chord. If at first you have trouble with the B♭ chord, try using B♭5 instead (just make sure to mute the high E and B strings).

BEAUTIFUL

Words and Music by Linda Perry
Recorded by Christina Aguilera

Dsus2 Dsus2/C Bm(add11) Bb Bb5 G Em Em7

TRACK #69: with vocals

TRACK #70: guitar only

Verse:

Dsus2   **Dsus2/C**   **Bm(add11)**   **B♭**
Ev'ry day is so wonderful, then suddenly   it's hard to breathe.

Dsus2   **Dsus2/C**   **Bm(add11)** **B♭**
Now and then, I get insecure from all the pain, feel so ashamed.

Chorus:

G   **Em**   **Dsus2**   **Dsus2/C Bm(add11)**
I am beautiful no matter what they say; words can't bring me down.

G   **Em**   **Dsus2**   **Dsus2/C Bm(add11)**
I am beautiful in every single way; yes words can't bring me down, oh no.

Em7   **Dsus2**   **Dsus2/C**   **Bm(add11)**   **B♭**
So don't you bring me down today.

Verse:

Dsus2   **Dsus2/C**   **Bm(add11)**   **B♭**
To all your friends, you're delirious, so consumed in all your doom.

Dsus2   **Dsus2/C**   **Bm(add11)**   **B♭**
Trying hard to fill the emptiness, the pieces gone, left the puzzle undone; ain't that the way it is?

Chorus:

G   **Em**   **Dsus2**   **Dsus2/C Bm(add11)**
You are beautiful no matter what they say; words can't bring you down.

G   **Em**   **Dsus2**   **Dsus2/C Bm(add11)**   **Em7**
You are beautiful in every single way; yes words can't bring you down, no, no.   So don't you bring me down today.

Bridge:

Dsus2   **Dsus2/C**   **Bm(add11)**   **B♭**
No matter what we do, no matter what we say, we're the song inside the tune, full of beautiful mistakes.

Dsus2   **Dsus2/C**   **Bm(add11)**   **B♭**
And everywhere we go, the sun will always shine, and tomorrow we might awake on the other side.

Chorus:

G   **Em**   **Dsus2**   **Dsus2/C Bm(add11)**
'Cause we are beautiful no matter what they say; yes words won't bring us down, oh no.

G   **Em**   **Dsus2**   **Dsus2/C Bm(add11)**
We are beautiful in every single way; yes words won't bring us down.

Em7   **Dsus2**   **Dsus2/C**   **Bm(add11)**
So don't you bring me down today.

B♭   **Dsus2**   **Dsus2/C**   **Bm(add11) B♭**   **Dsus2**
Don't you bring me down today.   Ah.   Don't you bring me down today.